Wernicke-Korsakoff.

Korsakoff or Wernicke-Korsakoff Syndrome Explained.

Wernicke-Korsakoff Symptoms, Causes, Treatment, Stages and Tests all covered.

By

Lyndsay Leatherdale

Published by IMB Publishing 2013

Table of Contents

Table of Contents

Table of Contents

Foreword

In April 2004, *The Evening Gazette* in Middlesbrough ran an article entitled, "Saved by the Circle of Friends." The piece told the story of a then 45-year-old Brendan Reilly, a man forever caught in the present.

Reilly's hard-drinking lifestyle robbed him of his ability to create new memories, a condition the article called "early onset dementia," but what it actually is, is Korsakoff dementia, the second half of a two-phase syndrome prevalent in alcoholics.

Patients with Korsakoff dementia, like Reilly, can generally remember things in the past with great clarity. They can carry on a lucid conversation and seem to operate with an average level of intellect — until a few minutes pass and they start repeating themselves.

Reilly, a resident in a nursing home thanks to the aid of two old school friends, hoped to recover enough to be more independent someday, but as one of those friends told the reporter, "His condition is a devastating thing for anyone to face."

That devastation can have an even more sinister face. In May 2013, Paul Bibby, writing for *The Sydney Morning Times*, detailed the death of 74-year-old Beverly Kain in February 2011.

Kain's son, Terrence David Kain, 48, strangled his mother. Suffering from alcohol-induced dementia, Terrence did not realize he was committing murder, nor did he have any memory of doing so afterwards.

Terrence was found guilty of manslaughter on the grounds of diminished responsibility. He received a four-year sentence, but the damage done to his brain by years of hard drinking that began in his teens makes him a "lifer." Neither Terrence Kain nor Brendan Reilly will ever fully recover.

Reilly is Irish, Kain an Australian. Both are products of cultures with a heavy emphasis on the social consumption of alcohol. They may or may not have suffered from Wernicke encephalopathy at some point in their drinking years.

Wernicke encephalopathy is regarded as a medical emergency that can be treated, usually with high doses of intravenous thiamine or Vitamin B1. This corrects the patient's mental confusion, abnormal eye movements, and unsteady gait in most cases.

If, however, these problems and others — principally a diminishment of cognitive function and severe short-term memory loss — become permanent, the patient has then entered the chronic phase of the illness, which is called Korsakoff dementia.

Korsakoff can, however, be caused by conditions other than alcoholism. Anything that robs the body of thiamine due to malnutrition can lead to the same effects. Such causes include, but are not limited to anorexia, hyperemesis gravidarum, and bariatric surgery.

For the person suffering from the condition, and for those caring for them, the long-term effects of Wernicke-Korsakoff are often tragic in the extreme.

Some patients recover sufficiently to function with some level of independence, while others need resident supportive care for the remainder of their lives.

In families already affected by the stress of years of alcoholic behavior, the switch to dementia caregiver can be brutal, straining remaining relationships to the breaking point.

Understanding the progression of this syndrome, how it is treated, and the nature of the damage it leaves behind are only pieces in the larger puzzle of managing that damage and from the wreckage, building some semblance of a new life.

One of Brendan Reilly's old schoolmates said of his friend's outlook on his condition, "He had a great sense of humor and worked through things cheerfully. This guy was so brave every single day."

Of himself, Reilly said, "I get very angry. Sometimes I sit thinking, beating myself up over what I've done. I've lost my short-term memory because of my drinking and that's my fault."

It is not the purpose of this book to discuss who is at fault, but only *what* is to blame — thiamine — or more specifically, the absence of thiamine.

Science cannot fully explain what thiamine does in the brain, only that it is essential to that organ, and to the function of nerves and muscles.

Thiamine seems to make all the electrical events that flow across these systems occur more smoothly and efficiently. Without thiamine, these same systems essentially short circuit and to an extent, shut down.

It is that potentially devastating chain reaction of deprivation and aftermath we will now explore.

Chapter 1) Wernicke-Korsakoff Explained

There is a great deal of confusion over the terms "alcohol-related dementia" and "Wernicke-Korsakoff Syndrome".

Over years of drinking, alcohol causes the brain to shrink, with concurrent diminishment in function across a broad spectrum of symptoms that present themselves not so unlike Alzheimer's.

Alcoholics of who have been drinking for a long time will have poor memory and attention span. They have difficulty in learning new tasks, reasoning, and problem solving.

The assumption is that their issues stem from alcohol, but the diagnosis is difficult, since they might also be alcoholics with vascular dementia or Alzheimer's.

1) How is Wernicke-Korsakoff Different?

Wernicke-Korsakoff is a two-phase condition that begins with an acute case of Wernicke encephalopathy that may respond to aggressive treatment with thiamine.

This medical emergency, if caught in time, can be resolved, especially if the patient stops drinking. If, however, the symptoms enter a chronic phase, the patient has passed into Korsakoff dementia.

Of those patients diagnosed with Korsakoff's, it is believed that about 25% will improve good function over two years. Some 50% see enough improvement to require only supportive care. Another 25%, however, will require residential caregiving for the remainder of their lives.

(It should be noted that exact predictions regarding recovery and improvement in a case of Korsakoff dementia are difficult to pin down. The second chapter of this book reviews a forty-year study with Korsakoff patients in which the numbers are less optimistic.)

While typically associated with alcoholism, it is critical to understand that any condition that robs the body of thiamine can cause Korsakoff syndrome.

These causes can be as varied as the constant vomiting present in pregnant women with hyperemesis gravidarum, to the aftermath of bariatric surgery.

Although Wernicke's encephalopathy was identified more than 130 years ago, there is still a great deal that is not understood about how this condition, and its companion, Korsakoff syndrome, so specifically damage the human brain.

Patients diagnosed with Korsakoff often sound completely normal, and would appear to be functioning with a good level of intelligence.

They cannot, however, form new memories, and are caught in the repetitive hell that is severe short-term memory loss, a fact with tragic consequences not only for their own lives, but for those of the people who love them and must care for them.

2) History of Wernicke-Korsakoff

In 1881, Carl Wernicke conducted autopsies on three patients. One of the subjects of study was a 20-year-old woman who attempted suicide by drinking sulfuric acid.

The resulting damage to her stomach caused severe pyloric stenosis, a condition affecting the valve leading from the stomach to the small intestine.

As a result of the projectile vomiting that followed, the young woman suffered pronounced dehydration and malnutrition with marked weight loss.

Her subsequent symptoms included:

- loss of muscle coordination
- mental confusion
- visual disturbances

Based on his post-mortem examination, Wernicke labelled this condition "polioencephalitis hemorrhagica superioris."

Over the next half of a century of study, the link between what became commonly known as Wernicke's encephalopathy and a nutritional deficiency was confirmed in multiple cases where patients were deprived of food.

The causes of this deprivation included intestinal blockages, malignancies, hyperemesis gravidarum, and alcoholism.

During World War II, when starving Allied prisoners of war were studied by their captors, the conclusion was that their symptoms resulted from a lack of thiamine, or Vitamin B1.

In such cases, if caught in time, nutritional therapy and intravenous doses of thiamine will lead to a resolution of the symptoms.

In cases where chronic alcoholism is a factor, however, nutritional treatment often does not work. These patients most generally progress to the chronic form of the disease called Korsakoff's dementia.

The Discovery of Korsakoff's Dementia

This neurological disorder Korsakoff's Dementia was identified in the late 19th century by a Russian neuropsychiatrist, Sergei Korsakoff.

As a continuation of Wernicke's encephalopahy, Korsakoff's is caused by permanent brain damage that, until recently, was believed to result in the patient requiring long-term institutional care.

Now, in some cases, rehabilitation programs can restore a limited amount of independence with a sufficiently supportive back-up system in place.

Korsakoff's does not present exclusively in alcoholics, however, and can occur as the result of any condition that deprives the body of thiamine.

In addition to profound short-term memory loss, Korsakoff patients also tend to confabulate, creating stories (often with wildly exaggerated details) to cover for their memory deficits.

The patients are not lying, but passionately believe what they are saying, and tend to become quite agitated when questioned.

3) Prevalence of Wernicke-Korsakoff

Worldwide, the prevalence of Wernicke-Korsakoff is thought to be about 1 in 1,000. Medical science admits, however, that this is an often under-diagnosed or misdiagnosed condition that may be mistaken for other forms of dementia.

In males, the condition's peak onset is between the years of 40-59, while females are most susceptible from ages 30-49.

When the percentages are isolated to the population of chronic drinkers, about 2% of alcoholics will be diagnosed with Wernicke-Korsakoff.

Those drinkers who engage in continuous, long-term consumptions of alcohol are at greater risk than binge drinkers. There appears to be no predilection based on race.

4) Signs and Symptoms

The signs and symptoms of Wernicke encephalopathy have long thought to be associated with a "classic triad" including:

- visual disturbances

- mental confusion
- an unstable gait

Only about 10% of patients diagnosed with Wernicke's actually suffer from all the symptoms in this triad, however.

The visual disturbances are now considered "ocular" in nature, and may include:

- double vision
- abnormal movements or nystagmus (rapid involuntary movement)
- eyelid drooping or ptosis

The lack of muscle coordination is most evident in the gait, which will be unsteady.

Memory loss and the inability to form new memories are both present, and hallucinations are a possibility.

Oddly, patients are often mentally alert, and exhibit good immediate comprehension with appropriate use of vocabulary and social skills intact.

5) Diagnosis and Tests

Typically, a diagnosis of Wernicke-Korsakoff is one of exclusion. The doctor will examine the patient and take a case history with the help of family and loved ones in an attempt to rule out such factors as:

- drug abuse
- closed head injury
- stroke
- brain tumor

If an accurate life history can be obtained, and long-term drinking is conclusively determined to be present or strongly suspected, the patient may be put on a "banana" bag. This IV, which is comprised of a yellowish liquid, contains:

- 100 mg of thiamine
- 1 mg of folic acid
- 3 grams of magnesium sulfate
- 1 ampule of multivitamin

The intent of this approach is to rapidly address underlying nutritional deficits.

Since ocular abnormalities resolve first in cases of Wernicke encephalopathy, if improvements become evident, the thiamine doses are then increased.

Although there has been some progress in detecting Wernicke reliably via MRI, treatment should never be delayed to schedule such an exam.

After IVs are started, blood work will typically be ordered to look at:

- liver function
- glucose levels
- blood arterial gases
- cholesterol
- and serum thiamine levels.

The test for thiamine remains the bellwether. When thiamine deficiency is confirmed, all subsequent treatments will be based on injections, IVs, or oral administration of the supplement.

Without treatment, or in very severe cases, Wernicke-Korsakoff carries a fatality rate of 10-20%.

6) Stages, Progression, Prognosis

Although estimates vary, it is believed that as many as 85% of Wernicke patients go on to develop Korsakoff syndrome.

They are left with long-term cognitive deficits, and many never get over the amnesiac characteristic of this condition. While this finding sounds particularly harsh, it is the reality of this progressive and pervasive cascade of symptoms and effects.

It is true that some patients do, in time, and with supportive care, develop the ability to form new memories, and to regain a degree of independent function.

Among those who are alcoholics, this improvement only occurs if they stop drinking. For those Korsakoff patients who are not drinkers – and for some who are – the outcome is still not guaranteed, which is one of the confounding aspects of this syndrome.

Consequently, a clear prognosis for a case of Wernicke-Korsakoff is highly unique per individual and often dependent on the quality and level of supportive care they receive.

Some research even points to a genetic susceptibility for the condition, which is, frankly, a complete wildcard in determining a long-term prognosis.

In cases where alcoholism is a factor, the new complication of providing caregiving for a person with functional dementia is often devastating for families already stressed to the breaking point.

If all family ties have been severed, the Korsakoff patient likely becomes a problem of the state. Budgetary issues and non-compliance in the absence of direct supervision typically complicate the individual's recovery to a greater degree.

Not surprisingly, in homeless populations where chronic drinking is prevalent, many individuals thought to be suffering from mental illness are actually living with undiagnosed cases of Korsakoff syndrome.

Determining the best supportive living arrangement for Korsakoff patients that provides an optimal chance of recovery becomes the dominant question that must be addressed by either loved ones or social service workers.

It is not surprising that many Korsakoff patients either "fall through the cracks" or suffer from the tangled bureaucracy of state-funded assistance programs.
Consequently, many never receive the help they need to achieve even a partial recovery. All too often, the presence of Korsakoff syndrome in this population is not discovered until the individual has died and an autopsy is performed.

Chapter 2) A Closer Look at Korsakoff Syndrome

In their book *The Wernecke Korsakoff Syndrome and Related Neurological Disorders Due to Alcoholism and Malnutrition* (1989), Drs. Maurice Victor, Raymond D. Adams, and George H. Collins relate their findings over 40 years of studying a group of patients with Wernicke-Korsakoff syndrome.

Although originally published in 1971, and arguably dated research, the findings of the authors' work is still enlightening due to both the breadth and length of the population whose progress they chronicled.

1) A Forty-Year Study

The core of the doctors' work involved a group of 245 patients, the bulk of whom were alcoholics. The study began between 1950 and 1952 at Boston City Hospital with 90 patients.

It was then continued from 1952 to 1961 at Massachusetts General Hospital with an additional 129 cases. The final 26 patients were added from 1963 to 1966 at Cleveland Metropolitan General Hospital.

Due to the geographic distribution and timespan involved, the research was not limited to any one racial or cultural group, nor was it confined to a given socioeconomic class.

Some of the patients were tracked over a period of 10 years or longer, and of the 245, autopsies were conducted on 82. In total, 186 patients survived the acute phase of the illness (Wernicke encephalopathy). Of those, 157, or 84%, developed Korsakoff syndrome.

a) Instances of Complete Recovery

Within the group of 157 with Korsakoff's, a total of 22 patients, or 21%, exhibited an almost complete recovery from their symptoms.

Even with this level of recovery, however, they had no memory of events directly preceding their acute illness.

They did, however, ultimately regain sufficient memory to be able to relate their past history. They could also remember what happened on a day-to-day basis, and they could learn new information.

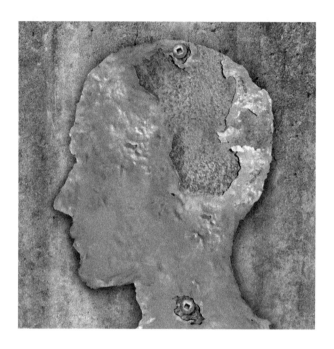

In 19 of those 22 patients, doctors rated the onset of their illness as severe. Therefore, the degree of their improvement did not correlate with mild initial symptoms.

In the larger percentage of these patients, recovery took place over a period of 1 to 3 months. In eight instances, however, the recuperation took as long as 10 months.

b) Cases with Significant Improvement

26 patients, or 25%, were judged to have shown significant improvement. While their recovery was still incomplete, these patients were able to carry out the tasks of daily living.

Members of this group continued to require varying degrees of supervision and support. Some did remain confined to institutions.

With this group, improvement manifested slowly and was prolonged over a period of three months to three years.

c) Patients with Slight Improvement

29 patients, or 28% showed only slight improvement. Within this group, 22 patients were observed for a period ranging from 2 to 10 years.

These individuals were only able to acquire the simplest skills and to retain very rudimentary information.

For instance, patients could find their way from their rooms to the dining hall in the hospital without assistance.

However, their ability to remember events on a day-to-day basis was severly limited.

When a single day had passed, they could recall only one thing that had occurred the previous day, and then only after prolonged examination.

d) Patients with No Measurable Improvement

27 patients, or 26%, showed no measurable improvement in neither memory function nor learning ability.

They remained severely impaired for life, and were incapable of functioning on their own in an independent living arrangement.

2) Presentation of Amnesia in Korsakoff

The authors concluded that the amnesia that presents with Korsakoff syndrome always has the same two features.

- **Retrograde amnesia**, which is the impaired ability to recall the information acquired over the many months or years preceding the onset of their illness.

- **Anterograde amnesia**, which is the impaired ability to acquire new information or to form new memories subsequent to their illness.

Additionally, the patient has little, if any, insight into the extent of their disability. Their behavior tends to be characteristically apathetic.

They do not have any spontaneity in their reactions or interactions, nor do they exhibit initiative. They tend to be completely indifferent to every body and every thing around them.

3) The Question of Confabulation

Although confabulation has traditionally been accepted as an integral factor of Korsakoff syndrome, it is a symptom that is exceedingly ill-defined.

The researchers in this study did not conclude that confabulation was consistently present, nor did they believe it was essential for a diagnosis of Korsakoff.

When confabulation is an aspect of the illness, it is most pronounced in the early days of the diagnosis. After receding for some time, confabulatory behavior tends to recur as the convalesence becomes more extended.

Patients will "run with" topics that involve their former occupation, or things they are used to doing.

For instance, if a patient was a frequent flyer, a casual question about the weather in relation to air travel might elicit a lengthly and involved commentary on:

- their airline of choice
- the amount of preparation for their trip
- events that occurred on the "journey"

- picking up the car at the airport
- the rising cost of travel by air

In other cases, however, the content of the confabulation is completely implausible to the point of being lurid.

There may be some vague connection with a past experience that triggers the tale, but otherwise the details are like Alice going down the rabbit hole.

Often patients will try to explain, perhaps for their own benefit, why they are living in a hospital setting. They may fabricate a detailed story about their daily commute, or insist that they are living "downstairs" and come "up" each day for treatment.

Typically this will be followed by assurances that they really do not have a problem, and that the doctors do not realize how much they are actually capable of doing.

When someone with Korsakoff's is challenged about one of these frabrications, they will respond with surprisingly logical answers for any inconsistencies in their story.

4) The Researchers' Diagnostic Criteria

According to the findings of this long-ranging study, certain factors must be present for a diagnosis of Korsakoff to be accurate. The patient must exhibit all of the following states:

- an alert and responsive state of mind

- awareness of his or her surroundings

- no serious defects in social behavior

- an understanding of what is being said

- ability to make accurate deductions from given premises

- problem solving in line with intact forward memory

In other words, the patient, for all practical purposes, appears to be lucid and normal. The degree of his or her deficits only becomes evident when the conversation or questioning has been of sufficient duration for the amnesia to become obvious.

Then, the signs will be repetition of thoughts or ideas already expressed, and incorrect answers to questions discussed over the past few minutes.

5) Nature of the Amnesia

Although the degree of amnesia will vary from patient to patient, there are distinct features. In some cases, the memory loss is startlingly severe.

Some patients, particularly at the onset of the condition, are so impaired that they cannot retain three simple pieces of information: the name of the person to whom they are speaking, the date, and the time of day.

This proves to be true even when the information is repeated literally dozens of times. Paradoxically, however, patients understand exactly what they are being asked to do and are generally puzzled why they can't seem to do it.

They will be capable of repeating each item correctly as it is presented to them. However, by the time the third item is supplied and repeated, they have no memory whatsoever of the first piece of information.

Over a period of weeks or months, the ability to memorize tends to improve to some degree. Even those patients that were most severely affected are able to learn simple things, like finding their way around the hospital. This limited capacity may, however, be the extent of the ability regained.

6) The Significance of Memory Impairment

For those of us who have functioning memories, it may be difficult to understand that the human ability to adapt to a new situation requires not only the acquisition of information, but also the ability to integrate that material with past experience.

The inability to acquire significant amounts of new information, coupled with the failure to merge that information with past experience, serves to render a Korsakoff patient helpless in society.

They are left with only the capacity, in many cases, to successfully perform habitual and routine tasks, but nothing of greater complexity.

The impairment of their past memories, however, like that of their ability to learn new information, is almost never complete, and is therefore both confounding and frustrating.

Korsakoff patients will retain "islands" of information, sometimes with great accuracy. However, they take those islands and relate them to one another without regard to logical or temporal gaps. They tend to build connections where none exist.

Additionally, the individual will telescope time. To them, an event that happened ten years ago happened just last year.

Everything else, however, appears perfectly "normal" including:

- vocabulary
- facility with language
- ability to use figures
- long-standing motor skills
- facial recognition of familiars
- social habits

They can accurately write from dictation, copy numbers, and draw simple figures on command like a clock face or a flower.

Researchers have not been able to pinpoint the determining factor behind what a Korsakoff patient forgets or remembers. This "Swiss cheese" effect remains a mystery.

7) Marked Changes in Affect

After the issues of amnesia and cognitive deficits, family members and friends find the marked change in the patient's affect one of the most difficult things with which to deal.

Korsakoff patients are highly apathetic and disinclined to do anything. Even making the effort to watch TV or speak to someone who walks in the room is too great. They are placid, bland, and detached, and exhibit no concern about their personal appearance.

Only in rare cases will the patient show resentment or dissatisfaction with his lot in life. Even then, they do so without conviction or a convincing display of emotions.

Even if the content of what they say could be characterized as an angry or irritable outburst, it will be lacking in the energy conventionally associated with those states.

Overall, it is difficult to elicit any type of emotional reaction from Korsakoff patients. When emotions are present, they are appropriate for the circumstances, but severely muted.

When directly questioned about their cognitive and memory deficits, a patient might acknowledge that they don't retain as much as they once did, but they tend to excuse away the seriousness of the problem.

Subtle Levels of Impairment

The agreeable and placid reaction of patients with Korsakoff, and the degree to which they can sound normal and, in some cases to acquire new information, can actually mask the degree of their impairment.

The researchers cited a number of cases in which an individual who was believed to be fully recovered returned to work, only to be dismissed from the position or quit within a matter of months, due to lack of performance.

In all cases, the employers, friends, and family of the affected person described the reason for their failure as a lack of interest and an inability to take initiative.

Essentially, when a Korsakoff patient has issues with self-insight, mood, and flat affect, these things don't tend to change even if memory and cognition do improve.

Some experts believe that the nature of the memory disorder with Korsakoff robs patients of their initiative because they can no longer effectively plan for the future.

8) Permanent Levels of Impairment

Even in cases where Korsakoff patients attain a functioning level of recovery, some degree of past experience will be forever lost to them.

No matter how hard the patient tries, those memories cannot be recaptured. Researchers have even attempted to elicit lost memories in Korsakoff patients under hypnosis with no success. It is as if those previous experiences simply never existed.

The mental symptoms that start with the confusion evident in a case of Wernicke encephalopathy and that, in the vast majority of cases, evolve into Korsakoff syndrome, follow a characteristic sequence.

The initial global confusion resolves, but it is replaced by a degree of amnesia that will, to some extent, be permanent.

Even in the face of thiamine treatment, the recognized standard protocol, approximately 80% of patients diagnosed with Korsakoff syndrome will never recover completely – regardless of their success in functioning on a day-to-day basis.

Chapter 3) The Thiamine Connection

Until this point, we have discussed Wernicke-Korsakoff almost exclusively in terms of its relationship to chronic drinking.

Most people have never even heard of Wernicke-Korsakoff, but if they have, it will invariably be in relation to alcohol use. To really understand the syndrome, however, it's important to move beyond this stereotypical association.

1) It's the Thiamine, Not the Alcohol

While alcoholism is the most identified "cause" of Wernicke-Korsakoff, the truth is that any condition that leads to a nutritional deficiency of thiamine in the body will have the same result.

Therefore, Korsakoff dementia could present in a pregnant woman with constant vomiting due to hyperemesis gravidarum, or in a child suffering the nutritional devastation of chemotherapy treatments for cancer.

a) Alcoholism Wages War on Thiamine

The reason Wernicke-Korsakoff is so closely tied to people with a drinking problem is the fact that alcoholics tend to have a very poor nutritional profile.

Additionally, heavy alcohol use impairs the ability of the small intestine to synthesize thiamine. Hepatic steatosis or fibrosis also reduces stores of thiamine in the liver.

Magnesium, which is an important "co-worker" with thiamine as a binding agent in cells, is also typically deficient in heavy drinkers. This additional insufficiency only raises the potential for thiamine-deficient conditions to develop.

For these reasons, regardless of the level of progression in a case of Wernicke-Korsakoff syndrome, getting the patient to stop drinking is imperative.

b) Korsakoff in Non-Drinkers

In recent years, however, the medical literature has been just as rife with cases of Korsakoff syndrome in bariatric surgery patients as in hardcore drinkers.

Consequently, a follow-up exam to check thiamine status is now recommended for these patients at the six-month mark, and is also critical for anyone recovering from a small bowel obstruction.

In some instances, the onset of Korsakoff after gastric surgery can take years, possibly indicating a cumulative effect of thiamine deficiency over time.

The culprit in these cases, and in other instances of non-alcohol induced Korsakoff, is identical to that seen in drinkers: severe thiamine deficiency.

2) What is Thiamine?

Thiamine was the first water soluble vitamin to be discovered. It was originally called aneurin and then Vitamin B1. Studies in nutritional deficiencies from the great age of sailing vessels ultimately led to the isolation of and understanding of thiamine.

History of Thiamine Research

In 1884, a surgeon general in the Japanese navy, Kanehiro Takaki, rejected the commonly accepted idea that beriberi

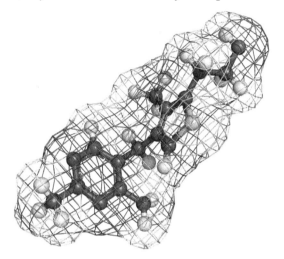

was caused by a germ. Takaki believed that diet was the true cause, and conducted a living experiment on a naval vessel that remained at sea for 9 months.

Rather than feed the sailors the typical diet of white rice, Takaki ordered a diet that included meat, milk, barley, bread, and vegetables. There were almost no cases of beriberi on the voyage.

Takaki wrongly assumed that the beneficial additive was nitrogen, but he was on the right track. Unfortunately, the Japanese navy found the improved diet too expensive, and went back to giving sailors nothing but rice. Beriberi-related deaths in the navy continued through the Russo-Japanese War of 1904-1905.

At that time, Takaki's approach was vindicated when it was discovered that the removal of rice bran in the polishing process caused beriberi. The connection to the grain itself was made in 1897 by a military doctor in the Dutch Indies, Christiaan Eijkman.

Eijkman experimented with feeding polished rice to fowl that subsequently developed paralysis. When the polished rice diet was discontinued, the paralysis disappeared. These experiments were confirmed by Gerrit Grijns in 1901.

Eijkman ultimately received the Nobel Prize in Physiology and Medicine in 1929. It was his work that spurred on the research that led first to the isolation of thiamine, and then the discovery of other "vitamins," so named by Casimir Funk in 1911.

The two scientists who actually isolated and crystallized the active thiamine agent in 1926 were also Dutch, Barend Coenraad Petrus Jansen and Willem Frederik Donath.

Thiamine was not synthesized until 1936, however, as a consequence of the work of an American chemist, Robert Runnels Williams.

3) Thiamine's Role in the Body

Thiamine plays an important role in the functioning of both the nervous system and the muscles. It is responsible for regulating the flow of electrolytes in and out of cells in these systems.
Electrolytes are ions that carry a positive or negative charge. They move through ion channels, which are proteins in the cell membrane that create tiny openings.

Only specific ions are allowed to pass in and out. The electrolytes carry nutrients into the cells and take wastes out, but they also conduct nerve impulses.

Without thiamine to regulate these impulses, many vital bodily functions can be interrupted including, but not limited to:

- the relaxation and contraction of muscles,
- the regulation of blood pressure,
- the function of our glands,
- and the pH or acid levels of bodily fluids including blood.

Additionally, thiamine is essential in enzyme processing, the production of hydrochloric acid for digestion, and carbohydrate metabolism.

4) Dietary Thiamine

The human body stores very little thiamine, only about 25-30 mg, primarily in the skeletal muscle, heart, liver, kidneys, and brain. Since our bodies do not produce thiamine, it must come from dietary sources.

Depletion occurs quickly, in less than two weeks, with serious consequences for the nervous, cardiovascular, and gastrointestinal systems. Of these, the nervous system is the most sensitive.
Major dietary sources of thiamine include:

- beef
- pork
- liver and organ meat
- eggs
- legumes (beans and lentils)
- kale
- asparagus
- cauliflower
- potatoes
- oranges
- milk
- brewer's yeast and baker's yeast
- nuts
- oats
- flax
- rice

- seeds (especially sunflower seeds)
- wheat and whole grain cereals

Of these items, the highest concentrations are found in yeast and pork. Most people get their dietary thiamine from cereal grains, with the most benefit derived from whole versus refined grains.

The difference in thiamine levels between whole and refined grains is striking.

- 100 grams of whole wheat flour = 0.55 mg of thiamine
- 100 grams of white flour = 0.06 mg of thiamine

In developed and industrialized nations, refined white flour and white rice products are typically "fortified" with thiamine, since much of the nutrient is lost during the refinement process.

In most countries the recommended daily allowance of thiamine is 1.4 mg, but therapeutic doses are much larger, and typically present no adverse reactions.

For the treatment of Wernicke-Korsakoff, the recommended thiamine regimen is 5-200 mg via intramuscular injection in five divided doses over a period of two days, plus 100 mg of intravenous thiamine.

Large doses of thiamine can sometimes cause drowsiness or burning at the injection site.

5) Beriberi

Apart from alcoholism, beriberi is the disease most commonly associated with thiamine deficiency. It primarily attacks the nerves and heart, and may be classified as:

- dry beriberi

In these cases the principal symptoms are peripheral neuropathy with impairment of motor, sensory, and reflex functions and severe muscle tenderness in the calves of the legs.

- wet beriberi

Presents as mental confusions, accompanies edema, atrophied muscles, and cardiac symptoms including tachycardia and congestive heart failure. (The trademark peripheral neuropathy will still be present.)

- infantile beriberi

When thiamine-deficient mothers breastfeed their children, the infants may exhibit cardiac beriberi with loud, piercing cries, tachycardia, and vomiting. Convulsions are common and death will occur if thiamine is not administered.

In all of these cases, the administration of thiamine leads to marked improvement within as little as 24 hours. Beriberi is rarely seen in the developed world today.

In East Asian countries, however, where polished white rice is a dietary staple, beriberi has been a long-standing problem.

With an improved standard of living in those regions, and the availability of a more varied diet, however, incidences of beriberi have begun to decline in recent years.

6) Broader Thiamine Deficient Conditions

Conditions other than alcoholism and beriberi in which thiamine deficiency can be a risk or a complication include the following. In each one, thiamine supplementation may be indicated.

- Alzheimer's Disease

Because Alzheimer's is a form of dementia, and serious thiamine deficiency causes Korsakoff's dementia, supplemental thiamine might offer some benefit.

From post-mortem examinations of brains affected with Alzheimer's, doctors have identified the lesions typical with the condition. Lesion-based damage is also present with Korsakoff dementia.

Given the tragic life consequences inherent in both conditions, thiamine supplementation may offer a clue to unravelling and ultimately addressing the scourge of Alzheimer's disease.

- Atherosclerosis

The regular use of thiamine may slow the build-up of plaque and cholesterol in the arteries. This build-up can lead to both stroke and heart attack.

Thiamine supplementation is a simple addition to a "heart" and "artery" healthy plan of preventive medicine.

- Cancer

Cancer creates greatly increased metabolic needs in the body, and often causes an overall state of malnutrition.

- Crohn's Disease

Although the case for beneficial supplementation for Crohn's patients has not been conclusively proven, decreased serum thiamine levels have been found in these patients.

- Diabetics

Thiamine supplementation can help to reduce typical diabetic complications involving the eyes, blood vessels, kidneys, and nervous system.

- Epilepsy

In patients with epilepsy, the administration of thiamine may help to improve both motor function and attention. While the data is limited at this time, the avenue of research is regarded as viable.

- Heart Failure

Severe and chronic thiamine deficiency can lead to heart failure, but conventional treatments for many heart conditions include the use of diuretics.

These drugs lower thiamine levels in the body, suggesting the need for thiamine supplementation as a corollary therapy.

- Hyperemesis Gravidarium

Pregnant women who are suffering from this chronic vomiting condition are often given thiamine as a precautionary agent, although the treatment does not, unfortunately, offer any relief otherwise.

- Total parenteral nutrition

Since TPN or intravenous feeding bypasses the usual digestive process, can, in the absence of supplemental thiamine, throw a patient into a non-alcohol induced episode of Korsakoff's.

Additional at-risk populations include patients with any gastrointestinal disease, anorexics, and those individuals with HIV/AIDS.

Although it is seen more rarely, there is also a genetic disorder called thiamine-responsive megablastic anaemia. This condition affects the transport of thiamine in the body or the conversion of thiamine into a usable, active form.

Special Section: A Genetic Component?

In 1977, J.P. Blass and G.E. Gibson, in an article for the *New England Journal of Medicine*, "Abnormality of a Thiamine-Requiring Enzyme in Patients with Wernicke-Korsakoff Syndrome," suggested for the first time that there might be a genetic predisposition in some individuals to suffer from thiamine deficiency.

This topic was taken up in 1993 by Peter R. Martin, Brian A. McCool, and Charles K. Singleton in "Genetic Sensitivity to Thiamine Deficiency and Development of Organic Brain Disease" published in the journal of *The Research Society on Alcoholism*.

The authors discussed the findings of autopsy studies that revealed that the brains of patients diagnosed with Wernicke-Korsakoff Syndrome showed demonstrable abnormalities including a reduction in both weight and the volume of white matter present.

The fact that only a subset of alcoholics ever progress to Wernicke-Korsakoff Syndrome was cited to bolster a genetic connection, as was the fact that identical twins show a much higher incidence of alcohol-related organic brain disease than fraternal twins.

The findings of the study suggested that thiamine deficiency may be associated with interactions of brain chemicals that are only evident when a state of relative malnutrition is present. This line of research did indicate some greater prevalence for the development of Wernicke-Korsakoff Syndrome in males.

Although the research is far from conclusive, this would explain why some long-term drinkers never develop Wernicke-Korsakoff, which typically presents itself in about 2% of the alcoholic population.

A growing body of literature suggests that many components of alcoholism are indeed genetic in nature, with Wernicke-Korsakoff potentially among them.

Further Reading:

For some of the most recent scholarly research in this area of investigation see:

Dick, DM, Cho, SB, Latendresse, SJ, Aliev, F, Nurnberger, JI Jr, Edenberg, HJ, Schuckit, M, Hesselbrock, VM, Porjesz, B, Bucholz, K, Wang, JC, Goate, A, Kramer, JR, and Kuperman, S. "Genetic Influences on Alcohol Use Across Stages of Development: Gabra2 and Longitudinal Trajectories of Drunkenness From Adolescence to Young Adulthood." *Addict Biol* (2013):

Edenberg, HJ, and Foroud, T. "Genetics and Alcoholism." *Nat Rev Gastroenterol Hepatol* 10, no. 8 (2013): 487-94.

Hendrickson, LM, Guildford, MJ, and Tapper, AR. "Neuronal Nicotinic Acetylcholine Receptors: Common

Molecular Substrates of Nicotine and Alcohol Dependence." *Front Psychiatry* 4 (2013): 29.

Hesselbrock, MN, Hesselbrock, VM, and Chartier, KG. "Genetics of Alcohol Dependence and Social Work Research: Do They Mix?" *Soc Work Public Health* 28, no. 3-4 (2013): 178-93.

Munn-Chernoff, MA, Duncan, AE, Grant, JD, Wade, TD, Agrawal, A, Bucholz, KK, Madden, PA, Martin, NG, and Heath, AC. "A Twin Study of Alcohol Dependence, Binge Eating, and Compensatory Behaviors." *J Stud Alcohol Drugs* 74, no. 5 (2013): 664-73.

Chapter 4) Treatment, Management and Care

There is little mystery to treating Wernicke encephalopathy. Thiamine treatment will reverse the condition if caught in time. Korsakoff, however, is more complicated, and may not even be diagnosed for several weeks. The patient must be completely alcohol free and passed the withdrawal stage before lingering cognitive deficits can be assessed.

At the point at which Korsakoff is identified as the problem, the focus becomes not so much a matter of a cure, but as how the condition will be managed, what degree of improvement is possible, and what level of caregiving or support the patient will require.

Almost all Korsakoff patients will need to be in an institutional rehab facility for some period of time. About 20% recover completely, but at least 80% will need long-term care at some level. Of those, 40% will continue to suffer from a shuffling gait for the rest of their lives.

1) The Human Equation

The level of frustration and heartache faced by loved ones and caregivers dealing with Korsakoff is palpable when reading their discussions on online support forums.

"My brother is in hospital at the moment, but they are looking at sending him out," writes one woman. "He has been assessed as not having capacity, and if I let the authorities have their way, he will be off to a nursing home or such."

Her request was for help finding a specialized care home in the hopes that her brother might recover some of his short-term memory. A few posts down, a daughter recounted her father's rapid deterioration after 40 years of drinking.

The man began by claiming he'd gone on day trips to New Zealand, had lunch with people long dead, or opened the door only to have strange animals wander into the room. He stopped drinking, but in three months time could no longer speak clearly, walk without assistance, or recognize his family.

Another frustrated daughter believed her father was drinking on the sly, in spite of his protestations to the contrary in the face of worsening mental and physical symptoms all pointing to Korsakoff's. "He denies that he has started drinking again during the last 8 years and has come up with bizarre excuses for each visit to hospital."

Others spoke of grappling with the concurrent demons of ongoing alcoholism and Korsakoff. "He is now drinking a lot," an embattled wife wrote. "His balance is nonexistent and his short-term memory loss is now down to 10 minutes." She bewailed the fact that she was receiving no practical help from her community alcohol or mental health team or the family's physician. "Soon it will be irreversible, and then what?" she asked.

One woman in the United States spoke up to say she had been living with Korsakoff herself for 10 years, but not as a consequence of alcohol abuse.

After gastric bypass surgery that ended in a partial bowel re-resection, she became thiamine deficient, developed Korsakoff, and had to spend two years in rehab learning to walk and "think again."

"I have to defend myself everywhere I go," she said, describing the assumption that her condition is the result of chronic alcoholism. "I can not [even] collect Social Security because Korsakoff's Syndrome is not a recognized disability."

Perhaps the most poignant message in the discussion thread came from a woman bewildered in the wake of her partner's diagnosis. "I have been with him for 6-7 years and I don't understand what will happen now," she said.

"Will he ever be able to live with me again and come home? No one is helping me understand this, and I don't know where to go for help. My partner does not understand what is wrong. All he wants to do is come home. The pressure is enormous just to take him home, but I know with his memory the way it is, I won't be able to cope on my own."

Unfortunately, the topic of long-term care for Korsakoff patients is addressed in a somewhat scattershot fashion in most medical sources. The confounding fact is that after the individual's condition has been stabilized with thiamine treatment, and the use of alcohol has stopped, overall health tends to improve.

The result is an adult who is physically sound, but mentally compromised. Long-term placement in a care facility is expensive, but after a year -- two years on the outside -- there will be little if any additional cognitive recovery. Whether or not an emphasis on conditioned learning will allow the person to live independently is highly subjective by case.

2) The Importance of Neuropsychological Assessment

Determining the specific nature of the cognitive deficit in a diagnosis of Korsakoff is crucial. A neuropsychological assessment should underly the development of any rehabilitation program, but the assessment may not be as sweeping as that which would occur in a case of mild to traumatic brain injury.

Typically, tests are administered to address the following areas of brain functioning and reasoning.

- attention span and memory

This should constitute a large portion of the deficit in most Korsakoff patients. Typically there is no language deficit and even mathematical reasoning will be intact. The person may test well on abstract and organized thinking, but not be able to recall the solution they've developed for more than a few minutes.

- general psychological adjustment

This component of testing looks at the way the person is dealing with their other cognitive deficits. Feelings of anger and frustration are common, as well as self-recrimination over years of drinking. Typically social judgment and level of appropriateness are not an issue.

3) Recovery Strategies

Many of the same strategies that are used in brain injury cases can be modified for use with Korsakoff patients under the guidance of therapy specialists. The goal is to create an optimal environment for maximum function.

It's important that any patient with a cognitive deficit recognizes when it's time to stop, rather than sticking with a task to the point that stress complicates their ability to cope. The brain isn't a muscle that is made stronger by harder work. Trying to do too much can actually hinder function rather than enhance it.

In order to facilitate learning, the person's life should be as scheduled as possible. Stress-relieving and pleasurable activities are also essential, especially in cases where alcohol is at the root of the cognitive damage.

Getting beyond self-blame and recrimination are also an aspect of recovery. Because Korsakoff is so life-altering and frustrating, patients can become easily discouraged and depressed.

It is important that family and friends are able to work with the trauma and recovery specialists to understand their own role in helping their loved one deal with Korsakoff. In families damaged by long-term alcoholism, this may mean healing old interpersonal wounds caused by the person's drinking.

Additionally, family members must have a place to share their own frustrations. These problems can range from anger over the initial cause of the disease to the fallout of dealing with insurance and government and medically-based bureaucracies.

4) Finding the Right Tools

Due to the major role memory deficits play in function, Korsakoff patients should benefit from a creative and comprehensive program of memory aid.
In a residential setting, for example, a patient might wear a beeper -- ostensibly for the benefit of the staff to prevent roaming off site -- but eventually the patient associates the beep with being in the wrong place. Similar strategies are applicable to home care.

The typical use of lists and labels is also indicated, but these systems must be simple or the patient must be taught to use them over and over again.

A notebook of vital daily information and instructions can be incredibly useful, if it can be designed in such a way that the patient actually remembers to carry and use it.

As an adjunct to any of these approaches, a NeuroPage or similar solution can be invaluable. This system was developed by the father of a young man who suffered from a brain injury. The device functions like any normal pager, but it sends programmed messages at specific times.

Commonly requested message types include things like:

- prompts to take medication
- orientating messages ("It's Tuesday at 3 p.m., you should be doing X.")
- meal and chore reminders
- social events
- family responsibilities
- bills due
- appointments

(See www.neuropage.nhs.uk in the UK for more information. A similar service is offered by AutoPage at www.autopagesolutions.co.uk . For similar information in the United States, see BrainLine.org.)

Care should be taken to select memory aids that have relevance to the patient, and to which they respond positively to further enforce their use.

Typically the decision about allowing a patient to live with some degree of independence is based on demonstrable abstinence of alcohol for a prolonged period, and a sufficient degree of memory to function safely in regard to daily living. The latter factor is especially crucial in regard to potentially dangerous chores like cooking.

Special Section: Wernicke-Korsakoff and the Elderly

In an article for *The Journal of Nurse Practitioners*, "Alcohol Use in the Elderly and the Risk for Wernicke-Korsakoff Syndrome," Christine Colella, Christine Savage, and Kyra Whitmer discussed the need for alcohol screening among elderly patients.

People aged 65 and older who have consumed alcohol in excess of the recommended levels for long periods are at risk for developing Wernicke-Korsakoff Syndrome even if they are not alcohol dependent. Unfortunately, in this age group, the conditions are more likely to be diagnosed on autopsy rather than in life.

The heavy use of alcohol over a lifetime creates a greater risk than that faced by people who begin to drink heavily after the age of 65, often in response to a traumatic life event like the death of a spouse.

Lifestyle questions during a health assessment are targeted at identifying early onset, heavy, at-risk drinkers by determining quantity, frequency, and duration of alcohol use.

Although there are many screening tools, positive answers to 2 or more of the questions on the CAGE questionnaire may indicate a problem:

- Have you ever felt you should cut down on your drinking?
- Have people annoyed you by criticizing your drinking?
- Have you ever felt bad or guilty about your drinking?
- Have you ever had a drink first thing in the morning to steady your nerves or get rid of a hangover?

According to the American-based National Institute of Alcohol Abuse and Alcoholism (NIAA), the recommended consumption for individuals aged 65 and over is:

- no more than 3 drinks in 1 day
- no more than 7 drinks in 1 week

By this scale, the total number of drinks in a week should not exceed seven.

It is important to understand that older individuals exhibit physiological changes that increase their susceptibility to alcohol-related health problems. These include:

- An overall decreased tolerance to the effects of alcohol in older people.
- A drop in the ratio of body water to fat.
- A diminishment of hepatic blood flow.
- Less efficient action of the enzymes in the body that break down alcohol.

The elderly also show a changed responsiveness to the intoxicating effects of alcohol. When people say they used to be able to drink more, they're right! As we age, it takes less alcohol to generate an intoxicated effect.

The NIAA defines a "standard" drink as 14 grams of pure alcohol. That translates out to about 0.6 fluid ounces or 1.2 tablespoons in American measurements.

Unfortunately, people tend to mix their drinks by perception, so that the common alcoholic beverage poured without a measuring device is 2-3 times the recommended size of a single drink.

When we drink alcohol, the substance generates an increased need for thiamine, but a vicious cycle is set in place in vulnerable people. Alcohol damages the lining of the intestinal tract or gut, so that thiamine is not properly absorbed from food.

Therefore, when we speak in terms of a deficiency, it's not just too little thiamine in the diet, but improper use of the levels of thiamine that are present due to malabsorption.

This problem can be even more pronounced among women because females metabolize alcohol differently. Women also have less available water in their systems, less lean body mass, and lower levels of the required enzymes to break down alcohol in the bloodstream.

Additionally, many elderly individuals take diuretics, which leaches more water from their system and increases their susceptibility to alcohol-related illnesses like Wernicke-Korsakoff induced thiamine deficiency.

In older people who have a long-term history of drinking more than the recommended levels of alcohol, even if they are not substance abusers, reducing or stopping drinking altogether and taking thiamine supplementation may be indicated.

Afterword

The progression of Wernicke-Korsakoff Syndrome, caused by severe thiamine deficiency, is a graphic illustration of the intimate role nutrition plays in our physical and mental well-being.

Although a condition long associated with chronic alcoholism, Korsakoff syndrome can manifest in anyone whose body is deprived of the thiamine it needs to function.

In the Foreword, I cited the extreme cases of 45-year-old Brenden Reilly, for whom every day starts afresh with little to no recollection of the previous 24 hours and that of Terrence David Kain who tragically murdered his own mother -- although he doesn't remember doing so.

In the developed world, the vast majority of cases of Wernicke-Korsakoff are tied to chronic long-term drinking, but in recent years more instances of this two-phase syndrome have begun to crop up in people who have sought bariatric surgery for weight loss.

For family and loved ones of people who have received a diagnosis of Korsakoff, the natural inclination is to find out how to "fix" it. Truth be told, medical science cannot answer that question.

Medical researchers do not completely understand the role thiamine plays in proper brain function, nor have they sorted out the "Swiss cheese" effect of the memory and cognitive loss that typifies Korsakoff.

With nutritional treatment and cognitive rehabilitation, about 20-25% of patients recover and return to their lives.

More than 80%, however, will live with some degree of impairment, including a flatter, less spontaneous affect in interacting with the world.

Certainly with supportive care and adequate memory aids, many will be capable of some degree of independence, but Korsakoff syndrome constitutes a long-term brain injury.

Sadly, it is not recognized as such by many insurance agencies or government entities responsible for dispensing aid and support.

The purpose of this text has been to shed some light on the underlying mechanics of Wernicke-Korsakoff, but I have no answers either.

My goal has been to give you the tools you need to ask better questions of the medical professionals and caregivers who will be a part of your loved one's life in the aftermath of a Korsakoff diagnosis.

If your loved one has been a long-term drinker, you may already have struggled through years of caregiving of a different sort. In your desire to help the Korsakoff patient, do not lose sight of your own need to talk with someone and to cope with the considerable stress of this situation.

Certainly where there is life, there is always hope. Rehabilitative therapies and the medical understanding of the human brain both continue to evolve.

The human brain has a much greater plasticity -- or ability to re-route itself -- than was once believed. Is this possible in cases of Korsakoff? There is no clear answer to that or to many questions surrounding this condition.

Without question, Korsakoff syndrome is a life-changing diagnosis, and one that affects not only the patient, but everyone in their lives.

On that journey, it is my sincere hope that you and your loved one find the answers you need.

Relevant Websites and Articles

Kennard, Christine. "How Does Alcohol-Related Dementia Differ from Alzheimer's?" HealthCentral. 30 April 2009.
www.healthcentral.com/alzheimers/c/57548/68445/alzheimer/

Korsakoff Syndrome, Alzheimer's Association
www.alz.org/dementia/wernicke-korsakoff-syndrome-symptoms.asp

Real Life Experience of Wernicke-Korsakoff Syndrome (Complicated by PTSD) Experience Project
www.experienceproject.com/stories/Have-Wernicke-korsakoff-Syndrome/1646201

Rebuilding Practical Skills After Having Wernicke-Korsakoff Syndrome, Alzheimer's Society
www.alzheimers.org.uk/site/scripts/documents_info.php?documentID=2140&pageNumber=2

"U.S. Drinks the Lowest Amount of Alcohol in the Developed World, Figures Reveal." Daily Mail, 17 February 2011.
www.dailymail.co.uk/news/article-1357892/U-S-drinks-lowest-alcohol-developed-world-figures-reveal.html

Wernicke-Korsakoff Syndrome Discussions. Patient.co.uk
www.patient.co.uk/forums/discuss/browse/wernicke-korsakoff-syndrome-2454

Wernicke-Korsakoff Syndrome Fact Sheet. Alcohol Concern.

www.alcoholconcern.org.uk/assets/files/Publications/Werni cke-Korsakoff%20Factsheet1.pdf

Frequently Asked Questions

While the text of this book goes into depth about Wernicke encephalopathy, Korsakoff syndrome, and related conditions, these are some of the most frequently asked questions by people just learning about these disorders.

Can you give me a brief explanation of Wernicke-Korsakoff Syndrome?

The syndrome is comprised of two disorders that are generally accepted as two stages of one condition. The first, Wernicke's encephalopathy, is caused by poor nutrition, specifically low levels of thiamine or Vitamin B1, which damages the brain.

Any condition or factor that causes a lack of thiamine can be an underlying agent for Wernicke's encephalopathy, but it is commonly associated with chronic alcoholism.

If untreated, Wernicke's leads to a second stage, Korsakoff syndrome or Korsakoff dementia, which is the presence of permanently altered learning and problem solving capabilities, to the point that independent living may no longer be possible.

What are the major symptoms of Wernicke-Korsakoff?

People suffering from Wernicke-Korsakoff seem, at first impression, to be fine. They know their friends and family. They can carry on a conversation. They cannot, however, form new memories. By a few minutes into a conversation, they will begin to repeat themselves because they no longer remember what has been said.

Other symptoms include poor muscle coordination, which manifests as an unsteady gait. The person will "confabulate," meaning they make up stories to cover for their lack of memory.

This is not lying. They believe everything they are saying, no matter how bizarre. This may or may not be accompanied by hallucinations, but the person will become confused easily.

There will also be changes in the eyes and with the vision including drooping eyelids, abnormal eye movements, and double vision.

Is it possible to treat Wernicke-Korsakoff?

In the early stages, patients with Wernicke-Korsakoff do often respond to an intense regimen of intravenous and oral doses of thiamine. The result will generally be a substantial improvement in their confused or delirious state.

Muscle coordination gets better, and vision problems resolve. Memory loss and cognitive function typically do not improve, however. In repeat or late-stage cases, thiamine may offer no benefit at all. In roughly 20% of cases, Wernicke-Korsakoff is fatal.

Why does alcoholism cause thiamine deficiency?

Heavy drinkers tend to have poor diets lacking in many essential vitamins, but alcohol particularly prevents the normal conversion of thiamine into its active and useful form, thiamine pyrophosphate.

Further, alcohol causes inflammation in the stomach often characterized by vomiting, which prevents the body from absorbing nutrients from the food that is consumed.

With these factors, and the added inability of an alcoholic's liver to store vitamins, it is almost impossible for an alcoholic to get or use the necessary amount of thiamine for proper nerve and brain function.

Who is affected by Wernicke-Korsakoff Syndrome?

About one in eight people with a dependence on alcohol are diagnosed with Wernicke-Korsakoff. In the general population, about 2 percent have the condition, which is most prevalent in men aged 45-65 with a history of heavy drinking.

The syndrome can manifest at an earlier age, however, and women are not immune. The group affected by Wernicke-Korsakoff is younger than those associated with both Alzheimer's and vascular dementia. It is not understood why some heavy drinkers do not develop Wernicke-Korsakoff, although genetics and diet likely play a role.

How is Korsakoff syndrome diagnosed?

The patient has to be alcohol free for several weeks to distinguish the effects of intoxication from those of Korsakoff syndrome. Withdrawal symptoms must also subside before a diagnosis can be made.

Typically a physical exam is conducted to rule out other conditions and lab tests will be performed. Psychological testing assesses the degree of memory loss and diminishment of cognitive ability. If the condition gets progressively worse, the diagnosis can be concurrent Korsakoff syndrome and dementia.

Can Korsakoff syndrome be treated?

Unlike vascular dementia or Alzheimer's, Korsakoff does not necessary get worse over time if the person stops drinking, started eating correctly, and receives high doses of thiamine. Some degree of improvement over the course of roughly two years is possible. Roughly 25% of those diagnosed with Korsakoff make a good recovery and return to some level of independent living, while about half make only a partial recovery and will continue to require support for the rest of their lives. The remaining 25% do not recover and generally need residential care.

Is alcohol-related dementia the same thing?

Alcohol-related dementia is not the same thing, but often that phrase is used interchangeably with Korsakoff syndrome, especially in any accounts of an individual case written for a general audience.

Alcohol-related dementia presents with broader symptoms that are a result of long-term alcohol abuse and are, in some ways, similar to Alzheimer's. This is, however, a difficult diagnosis even for the medical community, since the dementia could be caused by something other than the person's drinking.

Works Cited

Donnino, Michael W., Joe Vega, Joseph Miller, and Mark Walsh. "Myths and Misconceptions of Wernicke's Encephalopathy: What Every Emergency Medical Physician Should Know." *Annals of Emergency Medicine 2007* (50) 6: 715-721 (Accessed September 2013) www.synergymedical.org/acog/em/cola8/17681641.pdf

Gupta, Susham, and Warner, James. "Alcohol-Related Dementia: a 21st-Century Silent Epidemic?" *The British Journal of Psychiatry* 193, no. 5 (2008): 351-53.

Harrison, Rebecca A, Vu, Trung, and Hunter, Alan J. "Wernicke's Encephalopathy in a Patient With Schizophrenia." *Journal of General Internal Medicine* 21, no. 12 (2006): C8-C11.

Isenberg-Grzeda, Elie, Kutner, Haley E, and Nicolson, Stephen E. "Wernicke-Korsakoff-Syndrome: Under-Recognized and Under-Treated." *Psychosomatics* 53, no. 6 (2012): 507-16.

Mathew, Mariam, Mohan, Anita K, and Jacob, Poovathoor C. "Hyperemesis Gravidarum Complicated By Wernicke's Encephalopathy." *Neurosciences* 12, no. 3 (2007): 267-68.

McCormick, Laurie M, Buchanan, Judith R, Onwuameze, Obiora E, Pierson, Ronald K, and Paradiso, Sergio. "Beyond Alcoholism: Wernicke-Korsakoff Syndrome in Patients With Psychiatric Disorders." Cognitive and Behavioral

Neurology: *Official Journal of the Society for Behavioral and Cognitive Neurology* 24, no. 4 (2011): 209.

Ogershok, Paul R, Rahman, Aamer, Nestor, Scott, and Brick, James. "Wernicke Encephalopathy in Nonalcoholic Patients." *The American Journal of the Medical Sciences* 323, no. 2 (2002): 107-11.

Paparrigopoulos, Thomas, Tzavellas, Elias, Karaiskos, Dimitris, Kouzoupis, Anastasios, and Liappas, Ioannis. "Complete Recovery From Undertreated Wernicke-korsakoff Syndrome Following Aggressive Thiamine Treatment." *in vivo* 24, no. 2 (2010): 231-33.

Ramsey, Drew, and Muskin, Philip R. "Vitamin Deficiencies and Mental Health: How Are They Linked?" *Current Psychiatry* 12, no. 1 (2013): 37.

Rota-Bartelink, Alice. "Homeless Adults Living With Acquired Brain Injuries." *Parity* 23, no. 1 (2010):

Sechi, GianPietro, and Serra, Alessandro. "Wernicke's Encephalopathy: New Clinical Settings and Recent Advances in Diagnosis and Management." *The Lancet Neurology* 6, no. 5 (2007): 442-55.

Thomson, AD, Guerrini, Irene, and Marshall, E Jane. "The Evolution and Treatment of Korsakoff's Syndrome." *Neuropsychology Review* 22, no. 2 (2012): 81-92.

Thomson, Allan D, Guerrini, Irene, and Marshall, E Jane. "Wernicke's Encephalopathy: Role of Thiamine." *Practical Gastroenterol* 33, no. 6 (2009): 21-30.

Wilson, Kenneth. "Alcohol-Related Brain Damage: A 21st-Century Management Conundrum." *The British Journal of Psychiatry* 199, no. 3 (2011): 176-77.

Wilson, Kenneth, Halsey, Angela, Macpherson, Helen, Billington, Jane, Hill, Sharon, Johnson, Gavin, Raju, Keerthy, and Abbott, Pat. "The Psycho-Social Rehabilitation of Patients with Alcohol-related Brain Damage in the Community." *Alcohol and Alcoholism* 47, no. 3 (2012): 304-11.

Common Terms

A

abnormal eye movements - Any movement of the eye that cannot be controlled and that tends to be both rapid and repetitive in nature.

alcoholism - The compulsive urge to consume alcoholic beverages on a regular basis regardless of the negative effect of the behavior on a person's health, occupation, or interpersonal relationships.

amnesia - The blanket term for a number of conditions that present with memory loss.

apathy - A state of being in which an individual presents a flat affect to the world, devoid of either feeling or emotion, and with a marked disinclination for emotional arousal.

ataxia - A lack of co-ordination of the muscles that presents as a neurological symptom, in this case tied to an incident of Wernicke encephalopathy.

C

confabulation - A behavior in which an affected individual creates memories out of their imagination, typically to cover up for a cognitive impairment or the absence of a true memory. Instances of confabulation may be built upon fragmented actual memories, or they may be completely fictitious although presented in a logical and believable way.

confusion - When used in reference to a person's mental condition, confusion refers to a state of impaired thinking and an inability to retain a logical sequence of facts and events.

D

diplopia - The proper term to describe the ocular phenomenon of double vision.

K

Korsakoff's psychosis - A brain condition that presents as the second or chronic phase of Wernicke encephalopathy that is characterized by a progressive and often persistent loss of memory.

N

nystagmus - Movements of the eye or eyes that are both involuntary and jerky in nature.

O

ophthalmoplegia - A disorder of the eyes in which the muscles become paralyzed.

W

Wernicke-Korsakoff syndrome - A two-phase progressive syndrome prevalent in chronic alcoholics, but possible in anyone subject to a deficiency of Vitamin B1 or thiamine. In its chronic phase, Korsakoff's dementia, the syndrome is characterized by marked and often persistent memory loss.

Index

CPSIA information can be obtained
at www.ICGtesting.com
Printed in the USA
BVHW041533170321
602785BV00011B/1077

9 781909 151734